Books By Tahir Shah

The Writer's Craft
The Reason to Write
Workbook: Comprehensive, Volume I & II
Workbook: Fantasy, Volume I & II
Workbook: Fiction, Volume I & II
Workbook: Historical Fiction, Volume I & II
Workbook: Teaching Stories, Volume I & II
Workbook: Travel, Volume I & II

Novels
Jinn Hunter: Book One – The Prism
Jinn Hunter: Book Two – The Jinnslayer
Jinn Hunter: Book Three – The Perplexity
Hannibal Fogg and the Supreme Secret of Man
Casablanca Blues
Eye Spy
Godman
Paris Syndrome
Timbuctoo
Midas
Zigzagzone

Nasrudin
Travels With Nasrudin
The Misadventures of the Mystifying Nasrudin
The Peregrinations of the Perplexing Nasrudin
The Voyages and Vicissitudes of Nasrudin
Nasrudin in the Land of Fools

Travel
Trail of Feathers
Travels With Myself
Beyond the Devil's Teeth
In Search of King Solomon's Mines
House of the Tiger King
In Arabian Nights
The Caliph's House
Sorcerer's Apprentice
Journey Through Namibia

Teaching Stories
The Arabian Nights Adventures
Scorpion Soup
Tales Told to a Melon
The Afghan Notebook
Daydreams of an Octopus & Other Stories
The Caravanserai Stories
Ghoul Brothers
Hourglass
Imaginist
Jinn's Treasure
Jinnlore
Mellified Man
Skeleton Island
Wellspring
When the Sun Forgot to Rise
Outrunning the Reaper
The Cap of Invisibility
On Backgammon Time
The Wondrous Seed

The Paradise Tree
Mouse House
The Hoopoe's Flight
The Old Wind
A Treasury of Tales
The Tale of Double Six
The Forgotten Game
King of the Jinns
The Destiny Ring
Changing the World
Cat, Mouse
Frogland
Mittle-Mittle
Capilongo
The Princess of Zilzilam
The Singing Serpents
The Tale of the Rusty Nail
The Unicorn's Tear
The Clockmaker Who Travelled Through Time
The Fish's Dream
The Man Whose Arms Grew Branches
The Most Foolish of Men
The Shop That Sold Truth
Qwerty
Renaissance
The Man With the Tiger's Head
The Kingdom of Blink
The Wisdom of Celestine
Dream Soup
The Skeleton Factory
An Unexpected Gift

The Problem Exchange
The Pharaoh Code
The Monkey Puzzle Club
Liquid Time
Cat Dog, Dog Cat
Princess Pickle's Laugh

Anthologies
The Anthologies: Africa
The Anthologies: Ceremony
The Anthologies: Childhood
The Anthologies: City
The Anthologies: Danger
The Anthologies: East
The Anthologies: Expedition
The Anthologies: Frontier
The Anthologies: Hinterland
The Anthologies: India
The Anthologies: Jinns
The Anthologies: Jungle
The Anthologies: Magic
The Anthologies: Morocco
The Anthologies: Nasrudin
The Anthologies: People
The Anthologies: Quest
The Anthologies: South
The Anthologies: Taboo
The Anthologies: Teaching Stories
The Clockmaker's Box
The Tahir Shah Fiction Reader
The Tahir Shah Travel Reader

Research
Cultural Research
The Middle East Bedside Book
Three Essays

Edited by
Congress With a Crocodile
A Son of a Son, Volume I
A Son of a Son, Volume II

Screenplays
Casablanca Blues: The Screenplay
Timbuctoo: The Screenplay

BEYOND THE NEXT HORIZON

TAHIR SHAH

BEYOND THE NEXT HORIZON

APHORISMS BY WHICH A LITTLE BOY BECAME A MAN

TAHIR SHAH

MMXXIV

Secretum Mundi Publishing Ltd
124 City Road
London
EC1V 2NX
United Kingdom

www.secretum-mundi.com
info@secretum-mundi.com

Secretum Mundi Publishing edition, 2024

VERSION 26112023

BEYOND THE NEXT HORIZON

© TAHIR SHAH

Tahir Shah asserts the right to be identified as the Author of the Work in accordance with the Copyright, Designs and Patents Act 1988.
A CIP catalogue record for this title is available from the British Library.

Visit the author's website at:
TahirShah.com

ISBN 978-1-915876-40-9 (paperback edition)
ISBN 978-1-915876-41-6 (hardback edition)

All rights reserved. No part of this publication may be reproduced, stored in a retrieval system, or transmitted, in any form or by any means, electronic, mechanical, photocopying, recording or otherwise, without the prior written permission of the publisher.

This book is sold subject to the condition that it shall not, by way of trade or otherwise, be lent, re-sold, hired out or otherwise circulated without the publisher's prior consent in any form of binding or cover other than that in which it is published and without a similar condition including this condition being imposed on the subsequent purchaser.

This book is for all the dreamers out there, without whom the world would shudder to an immediate halt.

ONCE UPON A time, there was a little boy who felt different from all the other little boys he knew.

Unlike them, he couldn't understand the things the teachers were teaching in school. Nor could he catch a ball like the other kids, or sing in tune as they all did so perfectly, or memorize the endless volleys of nonsense fired constantly in his direction.

This little boy was no wiser nor more foolish than the other little boys.

Yet, a single word made him different from all the rest:

IMAGINATION

While all the other children thought precisely how they were told to think, and did precisely what they were told to do, this little boy did not.

Instead, he would slip into a magical realm of his own making – a realm in which absolutely anything was possible.

A day doesn't go by without me thinking of the twisting timeline of that little boy's childhood, and the fortress he constructed for himself from raw imagination.

And a day doesn't go by without me pondering how trial and tribulation might easily have swallowed him whole.

But they did not.

That's because the little boy in question learned to trust his imaginary fortress, just as he had learned to be safe there.

The more he trusted it, the more he realized it was the one corner of existence from where he could weave magic:

Magic conjured from the farthest limits of his own creativity.

This book is a collection of aphorisms by which the little boy learned, progressed, and grew into the man he is today.

No more than a handful of people will recognize its contents as being valuable.

I suspect that those who do were little boys and little girls isolated from all the others…

Isolated and scorned because they were different.

But, because they were different, they pushed themselves harder than others did – eventually conquering the immense challenges that lay on the path ahead.

Looking back to my own childhood, nothing was ever expected of me.

I was clumsy, messy, restless, dyslexic, and lost in a dream zone.

While those around me were expected to construct empires, I was left to my own devices.

Left to experiment.

Left to hope.

And, most of all, left to dream.

Since early childhood, I trained my attention on the distant horizon, ever curious to know what lay beyond it.

With time, and with experience, I developed ways to span the land and sea lying between me and the horizon.

Now I am ripened by life, and by adventure.

But the little boy still lives inside me.

The little boy still brimming with imagination.

The little boy different from all the rest.

The little boy who was destined to follow his dreams, and to venture far beyond the next horizon.

Tahir Shah

A LIFE
WITHOUT STEEP
LEARNING CURVES
IS NO LIFE
AT ALL

CREATE FOR
YOURSELF —
NOT TO GAIN
THE ATTENTION
OF OTHERS

NEVER
EVER EVER EVER
LISTEN TO ANYONE
WHO HOLDS
YOU BACK

TRAVEL
FAR
TO
FIND
YOURSELF

A
STRAIGHT
ROAD NEVER
LED ANYWHERE
WORTH GOING

DON'T EVER
QUESTION
WHETHER
YOU HAVE
THE SKILL

MARCH TOWARDS
THE NEXT HORIZON
LEAVING ALL
NAYSAYERS
IN YOUR WAKE

PERFECT
YOUR CRAFT
THEN SPIN
YOUR
GOLD

PRODUCE
PRODUCE
PRODUCE

ORIGINALITY
IS THE
SECRET
TO
SUCCESS

DO
THE WORK
YOU ARE IN
THE MOOD
TO DO

DON'T TALK
ABOUT WHAT
YOU ARE
PLANNING —
DO IT INSTEAD

THE BEST
IDEAS ARE
STEWED WELL
OVER THE
FLAME OF TIME

A FULL SPECTRUM
OF CIRCUMSTANCES
MAKES FOR
THE MOST
INTERESTING LIFE

KEEP
CONTROL
OF ANYTHING
THAT BEARS
YOUR NAME

PUSH
YOURSELF
HARDER
THAN YOU
PUSH OTHERS

A JOURNEY OF
GREAT DISCOVERY
CAN TAKE PLACE
ON A
SINGLE STREET

DILIGENCE
NOT
GENIUS
LEADS
TO TRIUMPH

THE MAGIC LIES
AT THE
CONFLUENCE OF
PEOPLE, PLACES
AND IDEAS

DRINK
FROM THE WELL
BEYOND
THE NEXT
HORIZON

CLOSE
YOUR EYES
AND SEE WHAT
IS HIDING IN
PLAIN SIGHT

LIFE IS A FULL RADIO
BANDWIDTH —
DON'T LIMIT
YOURSELF TO A
SINGLE STATION

CROSS OCEANS
IN A SHIP
CRAFTED FROM
YOUR OWN
IMAGINATION

PLACE
ULTIMATE TRUST
IN NO ONE
BUT
YOURSELF

NOTHING IS LESS
IMPORTANT THAN
BODY IMAGE —
WHAT COUNTS IS
MIND IMAGE

TOUCH WITH YOUR EYES
SMELL WITH YOUR EARS
SEE WITH YOUR NOSE
HEAR WITH YOUR TONGUE
TASTE WITH YOUR HANDS

A BOOK
WRITES ITSELF
WHEN YOU SIT
BACK AND
ENJOY THE RIDE

NO ADVENTURE
OF ANY WORTH
ENDED IN A
SINGLE
DESTINATION

THE WISDOM OF FOOLS
IS FAR MORE
VALUABLE THAN
THE FOOLISHNESS
OF THE WISE

EVEN THOUGH
WE FAIL TO
RECOGNIZE IT
WATER HAS
A TASTE

THE
ANSWER
TO A
FOOL IS
SILENCE

A TINY GRAIN
OF SAND
IS A FRAGMENT
OF A
MIGHTY MOUNTAIN

TO LISTEN TO THE
STORY OF THE OCEAN
IS TO LEARN
THE LANGUAGE
OF THE WAVES

A STORY
TELLS
OF US
AS WE TELL
OF IT

THINK
MUCH
BIGGER
THAN
BIG

YOU HAVE NO HOPE OF
PROGRESS IF YOU FLOAT
ON A LAKE OF DOUBT —
DRAIN THE LAKE AND
WALK TO THE SHORE

EXPERIENCE
IS THE
ONLY TOOL
VITAL FOR
SUCCESS

WHO CAN SAY
WHAT WONDERS
FISH BEHOLD
IN THEIR
DREAMS?

EMBRACE
THE
COURAGE
REQUIRED
TO FAIL

BELIEVING IN
MONSTERS
UNDER THE BED
DEVELOPS THE
IMAGINATION

NOT ALL FRIENDS
ARE DESTINED TO
JOURNEY WITH YOU
TO WHERE THE RIVER
MEETS THE SEA

INSANITY
AND GENIUS
ARE CUT
FROM THE VERY
SAME CLOTH

FORGET TRYING
TO BE
SOMEONE ELSE
AND START
BEING YOURSELF

ANONYMOUS
CHARITY
IS SWEETER
THAN
WILD HONEY

TRY TO
IMAGINE HOW
THE BLIND
EXPERIENCE
YOU

OVERTHINKING
IS AKIN TO
DISMANTLING
A MECHANICAL
CLOCK

WHEN HOBBLED
BY WOES
HOW CAN A CAMEL
EXPECT TO REACH
THE HORIZON?

NEVER
PIGGYBACK
ON THE
ABILITIES OF
OTHERS

KEEP PERSPECTIVE —
OUR HOME IS
A LUMP OF ROCK
SPINNING IN THE
UNIVERSE

IMPROVING
ONESELF
IS
BEST DONE
FROM WITHIN

DESPITE
ONE'S HOPES
MISERLY
PEOPLE
RARELY CHANGE

A
PASSENGER
CAN'T CHOOSE
THEIR
DESTINATION

TO BE
A WRITER
YOU NEED ONE THING
AND ONE THING ALONE:
MENTAL SPACE

NO MIRROR
REFLECTS
ANYTHING
DEEPER THAN
THE SURFACE

STUPIDITY
OCCASIONALLY
HAS
ITS
USES

THE NORTHERN
BORDER OF ONE
IS THE
SOUTHERN BORDER
OF ANOTHER

LAY DOWN
STRONG
FOUNDATIONS
AND BUILD
UPON THEM

ONLY A FOOL
IMAGINES
THEIR VERSION
OF REALITY
IS SUPERIOR

THERE IS NO SHARPER
WAY TO UNDERSTAND
A COUNTRY THAN
BY LISTENING TO
ITS STORIES

DON'T BE AFRAID
TO BATHE IN
THE WATER OF
SELF-LOVE
ONCE IN A WHILE

FEAR
SAVES LIVES
WHILE
BRAVERY
ENDS THEM

LEARNING THROUGH
PLAY SHARPENS
THE MIND —
LEARNING THROUGH
REPETITION DULLS IT

A LANGUAGE
SPOKEN BY A
SINGLE MOUTH
IS OF
LIMITED USE

IF THE BRAINS
OF HUMANS WERE
HALF THE SIZE
OUR PLANET'S FUTURE
WOULD BE SECURE

SALT CAN MAKE
PLAIN FOOD
DELICIOUS AND
DELICIOUS FOOD
INEDIBLE

SOCIAL MEDIA —
THE GREATEST
EXPERIMENT ON
HUMAN SOCIETY
IN HISTORY

GREED
MAKES US
WHO WE ARE
AND WHO WE
OUGHT NOT TO BE

NEVER GO
THROUGH THE
FRONT DOOR
IF THERE'S ANOTHER
DOOR AT THE BACK

LOVE THE MOON
BUT REMEMBER
IT IS THE SUN
THAT PROVIDES
HER LIGHT

ENCOURAGEMENT
IS WORTH
TWICE
ITS WEIGHT
IN GOLD

TRAVEL THROUGH
A STORY
TO THE LIMITS
OF YOUR OWN
IMAGINATION

STOP
QUESTIONING
YOUR ABILITY
AND GET DOWN TO
CREATING YOUR WORK

THOSE
WHO GAVE
US LIFE
LIVE
WITHIN US

MOST OF LIFE'S
PROBLEMS COULD
BE SOLVED BY
RANDOM ACTS
OF KINDNESS

DEVELOPING
A PIPELINE OF WORK
AND OF IDEAS
WILL CREATE
YOUR FUTURE

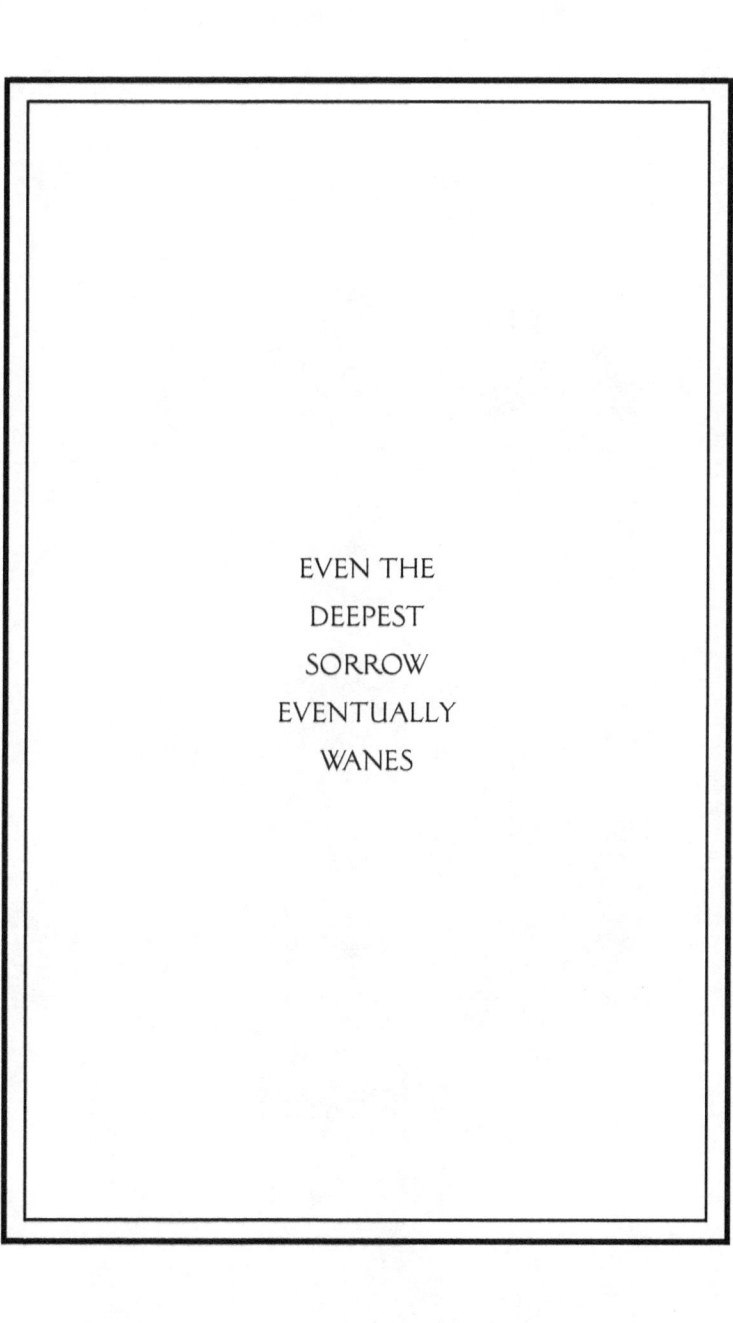

EVEN THE
DEEPEST
SORROW
EVENTUALLY
WANES

AMBITION
IS THE
DISTANT HORIZON
AND DILIGENCE IS
THE FOOTPATH

MOST PEOPLE
DON'T NEED
GLASSES SO MUCH
AS THEY DO
FRESH EYES

ASK YOURSELF
THE SAME QUESTION
OVER AND OVER —
AM I READY TO
CHANGE DIRECTION?

WORKING WITH
INTELLIGENT PEOPLE
IS LIKE
COOKING WITH
SHARP KNIVES

A GOOD BOOK
IS AS MAGICAL
AS THE WAND
IN A
SORCERER'S HAND

VERY LITTLE
OF WHAT WE
CLING TO
AS HUMANS
ACTUALLY EXISTS

THERE IS ALWAYS
HOPE —
EVEN WHEN
THERE IS
NO HOPE AT ALL

WORK THE MUSCLE
THAT IS ONE'S
CREATIVITY
AND
MIRACLES OCCUR

GIVE FAR MORE
THAN YOU TAKE
AND TAKE
ONLY WHAT
YOU NEED

LEAVE MONEY YOU
FIND IN THE STREET
FOR SOMEONE WHO
NEEDS IT MORE
THAN YOU

EXTEND
THE TIMELINE
AND
SOLUTIONS READILY
PRESENT THEMSELVES

PARK
YOUR WORRIES
AND FOCUS
ON WHAT
REALLY MATTERS

WHEN ENCOUNTERING
THOSE WITH A
CHRONIC NEED FOR
PRAISE, PRAISE THEM
AND MOVE ON

COLLABORATE WITH
PEOPLE WHO
HAVE A DIFFERENT
SKILL SET
TO YOURSELF

AVOID CRUEL PEOPLE
AS THEIR
SHORTCOMING
CAN NEVER
BE REMEDIED

GLIMPSE DETAILS
WITH ONE EYE
AND THE
BIG PICTURE
WITH THE OTHER

A SERPENT
MAY SLOUGH
ITS SKIN
YET IT REMAINS
A SERPENT

INVENTIVENESS
IS THE
BEST MEDICINE
FOR AN
UNSETTLED MIND

NO
MORSEL OF
LIFE ADVICE
IS TOO
INSIGNIFICANT

APPRECIATE
GRATITUDE
RIGHT DOWN
TO THE MARROW
OF YOUR BONES

NEVER EVER THINK
ABOUT GIVING UP ON
SOMETHING THAT'S
COMMANDED YOUR
FULL ATTENTION

TAKE TIME
TO CONSTRUCT
THE VERY FINEST
VERSION OF
YOURSELF

BE
SOMEONE
WHO
REPAYS
DEBTS

DON'T LIVE
SOMEONE ELSE'S
AMBITIONS —
LIVE YOUR
OWN

THE SMALLEST
ANT
CAN DREAM
THAT IT IS AN
ELEPHANT

A MOTH FLIES
NOT TO THE FLAME
BUT TO THE
DARKNESS
BEHIND IT

HUMANITY'S
CHALLENGE
BEGAN WITH
THE INVENTION
OF THE WHEEL

MUCH TRAVEL
IS NEEDED
BEFORE
A RAW MAN
IS RIPENED

NOTHING
IS QUITE SO
INEXPLICABLY
HUMAN AS
LAUGHTER

THE FEAR OF FAILURE
IS FAR MORE
UNIVERSAL
THAN THE
FEAR OF SUCCESS

SEARCH OUT
HEROES
AND LIVE
BY THEIR
EXAMPLE

AN ADVENTURE
IS OF
NO MERIT
UNLESS IT HAS
TESTED YOU

STORIES
ARE THE
COMMUNAL
CURRENCY OF
HUMANITY

WHAT WAS
IMPOSSIBLE
BECOMES POSSIBLE
BY BELIEVING
ABSOLUTELY

REAL
TRAVEL
IS ALL
ABOUT
LONELINESS

REACH FOR THE STARS
AND ALLOW
YOUR IMAGINATION
TO FIND
ITS OWN PATH

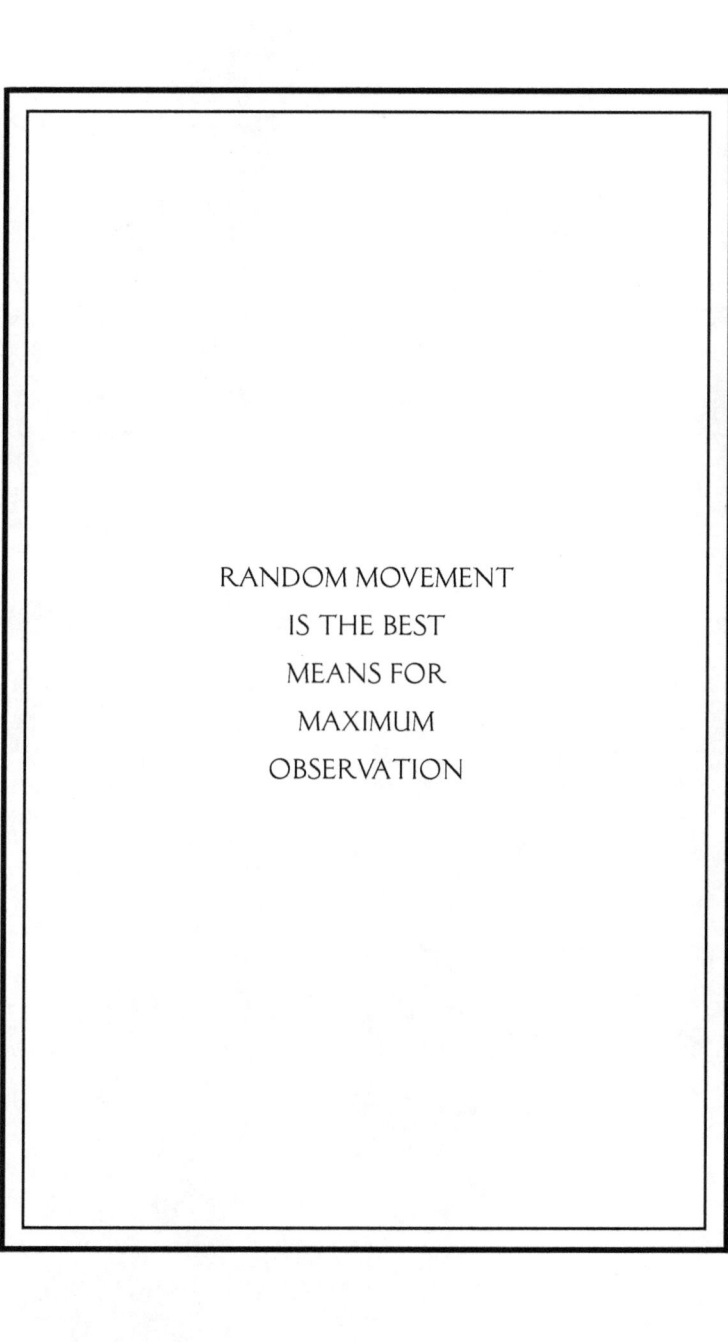

GROW
INTO
WHO YOU
ARE DESTINED
TO BE

FOLKTALES
ARE NOT
HELD BACK
BY WHAT IS
FALSE OR TRUE

IMAGINATION LIVES
DEEP INSIDE US ALL —
A SPARK
WAITING TO SET
A TOUCHPAPER ALIGHT

THE TASTE FOR
GLORY CAN MAKE
ORDINARY MEN
BEHAVE IN
EXTRAORDINARY WAYS

LEARN
TO BE
YOUR
OWN
BEST FRIEND

A
ZIGZAG STRATEGY
IS USUALLY
THE BEST WAY
TO FLOURISH

DON'T BE
AFRAID
TO DWELL
IN
NO MAN'S LAND

BE
WORTHY
OF
YOUR
FUTURE

THE MASTERY OF
ELEMENTARY TASKS
IS A
NECESSITY
FOR ACHIEVEMENT

THERE IS NOTHING
LIKE A QUEST
FOR GETTING
YOUR
BLOOD PUMPING

REAL WRITERS HAVE TO
DESCEND INTO THE
DARKNESS IF THEY
HOPE TO REACH
THE MAGIC ZONE

WHAT IS
IMPORTANT IS
HOW A STORY
MAKES YOU
FEEL INSIDE

THE CONTENT
OF A LIFE
IS MORE
IMPORTANT
THAN ITS LENGTH

AS A WRITER
MY DESTINATION IS
THE LAND OF
TRUE-TO-ONESELF-
CREATIVITY

ARTIFICIAL
INTELLIGENCE
IS AS ARTIFICIAL
AS IT IS
UNINTELLIGENT

THE UNFULFILLED
LISTEN
TO OTHERS
RATHER THAN
TO THEMSELVES

NEVER EVER
FORGET HOW
INCREDIBLY
LUCKY
YOU ARE

ISOLATED EVENTS
HOLD THE
KEY TO
GREAT
BREAKTHROUGHS

NEITHER
SUCCESS NOR
GOOD FORTUNE
ARE FORGED
BY ACCIDENT

REGARD
A SITUATION
FROM EVERY
CONCEIVABLE
ANGLE

WHEN CHOOSING
A GIFT —
GIVE TWICE
WHAT YOU HAD
PLANNED

DREAM
AS THOUGH
YOUR LIFE
DEPENDED
UPON IT

A MAN
WHO EMBARKS
ON A JOURNEY
MUST KNOW WHEN
TO END IT

A REQUEST

If you enjoyed this book, please review it on your favourite online retailer or review website.

Reviews are an author's best friend.

To stay in touch with Tahir Shah, and to hear about his upcoming releases before anyone else, please sign up for his mailing list:

✉ http://tahirshah.com/newsletter

And to follow him on social media, please go to any of the following links:

🐦 http://www.twitter.com/humanstew

📷 @tahirshah999

ƒ http://www.facebook.com/TahirShahAuthor

▶ http://www.youtube.com/user/tahirshah999

𝑃 http://www.pinterest.com/tahirshah

g https://www.goodreads.com/tahirshahauthor

http://www.tahirshah.com

www.ingramcontent.com/pod-product-compliance
Lightning Source LLC
LaVergne TN
LVHW041248080426
835510LV00009B/637